COVENENT KEYS TO ANSWERED PRAYERS

And this is the confidence that we have in him that, if we ask any thing according to his will, he heareth us.

1 John 5:14

by
Franklin N. Abazie

Covenant Keys to Answered Prayers
COPYRIGHT 2016 BY Franklin N Abazie
ISBN: 978-1-945133-23-7

All right reserved. This book or any portion thereof may not be reproduced or used in any manner whatsoever without the express written permission of the publisher, except for the use of brief quotations in a book review. All Bible quotes are from King James Version and others as noted.

Published by: F N ABAZIE PUBLISHING HOUSE—aka, Empowerment Bookstore

That I may publish with the voice of thanksgiving and tell of all thy wondrous works.
Psalms 26:7

To order additional copies, wholesales or booking call:
the Church office (973-372-7518)
or Empowerment Bookstore Hotline (973-393-8518)

Worship address:
343 Sanford Avenue, Newark, New Jersey 07106
Administrative Head Office address:
33 Schley Street Newark New Jersey 07112
Email: pastorfranknto@yahoo.com
Website www.fnabaziehealingministries.org
Publishing House: www.fnabaziepublishinghouse.org

This book is a production of F N Abazie Publishing House. A publication Arms of Miracle of God Ministries 2016.
First Edition

CONTENTS

THE MANDATE OF THE COMMISSION...................iv
ARMS OF THE COMMISSION.................................v
INTRODUCTION..vi
CHAPTER 1
How Do I Pray?...1
CHAPTER 2
The Prayer That Works..17
CHAPTER 3
The Benefits of Prayer...38
CHAPTER 4
Prayer of Salvation...54
CHAPTER 5
About the Author...63

THE MANDATE OF THE COMMISSION

"The moment is due to impact your world through the revival of the healing & miracle ministry of Jesus Christ of Nazareth.

"I am sending you to restore health unto thee and I will heal thee of thy wounds, said the Lord of Host."

ARMS OF THE COMMISSION

1) F N Abazie Ministries—Miracle of God Ministries (Miracle Chapel Intl)

2) F N Abazie TV Ministries: Global Television Ministry Outreach

3) F N Abazie Radio Ministries: Radio Broadcasting Outreach

4) F N Abazie Publishing House: Book Publication

5) F N Abazie Bible School: also called Word of Healing Bible School (W.O.H.B.S.)

6) F N Abazie Evangelistic Ass: Miracle of God Ministries: Global Crusade

7) Empowerment Bookstore: Book distribution

8) F N Abazie Helping Hands: Meeting the Help of the Needy Worldwide

9) F N Abazie Disaster Recovery Mission: Global Disaster Recovery

10) F N Abazie Prison Ministry: Prison Ministry For All Convicts "Second Chance"

Some of our ministry arms are awaiting the appointed time to commence.

INTRODUCTION

And this is the confidence that we have in him, that, if we ask any thing according to his will, he heareth us.
1 John 5:14

Quite frankly, in my own opinion prayer is a noble thing to do in life. The act of praying is so powerful that it is the bridge of hope for the believer. So many prayerless folks are drowning into frustration and depression because of lack of a prayer life. We all must rise up to pray like never before because the enemy is at loose. Unless we provoke angelic assistance through our prayer petitions, we will forever remain the prey and vulnerable to the adversary—the devil.

Call unto me, and I will answer thee, and show thee great and mighty things, which thou knowest not.
Jeremiah 33:3

It's vital for us to understand that unless we pray without ceasing, we will never experience great and mighty things in life. *"Pray without ceasing."* (1 Thessalonians 5:17) Everyone that desires to experience God with an encounter must be in command of the Biblical-approved method to pray correctly to God.

Until now you have not asked for anything in my name. Ask and you will receive, and your joy will be complete.
John 16:24

And he went a little farther, and fell on his face, and prayed, saying, O my Father, if it be possible, let this cup pass from me: nevertheless not as I will, but as thou wilt.
Matthew 26:39

Remember...

And this is the confidence that we have in him, that, if we ask any thing according to his will, he heareth us.
1 John 5:14

And he was withdrawn from them about a stone's cast, and kneeled down, and prayed, Saying, Father, if thou be willing, remove this cup from me: nevertheless not my will, but thine, be done.
Luke 22:41-42

Jesus is the yardstick for us to understand the approved method to pray. In my own understanding, every kingdom prayer that proclaims and declares the will of the Father is acceptable to God.

And as he prayed, the fashion of his countenance was altered, and his raiment was white and glistering.
Luke 9:29

A careful examination of the life of Jesus Christ will prove to you that in public, His prayers were mostly short prayers that manifested with power, glory, authority, healing and miracles. These powerful prayers were precise and accurate. Although Jesus prayers were very short in public, these short, powerful prayers were the result of His private long prayer time with the Father. In private, for example, Jesus prayed long prayers. Jesus prayed all night prayers to provoke power from the heavenly places.

Unless we all understand the secret to answered prayers, we are deceiving ourselves.

Watch and pray, that ye enter not into temptation:
the spirit indeed is willing, but the flesh is weak.
He went away again the second time, and prayed,
saying, O my Father, if this cup may not pass away from
me, except I drink it, thy will be done. And he came and
found them asleep again: for their eyes were heavy.
And he left them, and went away again,
and prayed the third time, saying the same words.
Matthew 26:41-44

In this publication, we will be revealing what the Holy Spirit is saying to us all with significant emphasizes on covenant keys to answered prayers. It is written, *"O thou that hearest prayer, unto thee shall all flesh come."* (Pslams 65:2)

And these signs shall follow them that believe;
In my name shall they cast out devils;
they shall speak with new tongues.
Mark 16:17

As believers, we're spiritual law enforcement officers with a warrant for the arrest of the devil. But it must be enforced through strong warfare prayers. I believe and trust God that as you go through these pages, every prevailing voice raising a counter motion against your elevation will be silent, in the name of Jesus.

"For we wrestle not against flesh and blood,
but against principalities, against powers,
against the rulers of the darkness of this world,
against spiritual wickedness in high places
Ephesians 6:12

"Life is a warfare and not a fun fare." Unless we engage the enemy in battle through ceaseless prayer, night and day, we will never prevail against the old devil. We must all be armed with violent prayer strategies to wage war against the devil every day and in every place. *"Put on the whole armour of God that ye may be able to stand against the wiles of the devil."* (Ephesians 6:11)

Come with me as we unfold what the Holy Spirit is saying through the pages of this book: COVENANT KEYS TO ANSWERED PRAYERS.
Happy Reading!

BIBLICAL PRINCIPLES TO PRAYER

And when thou prayest, thou shalt not be as the hypocrites are: for they love to pray standing in the synagogues and in the corners of the streets, that they may be seen of men. Verily I say unto you, They have their reward.

But thou, when thou prayest, enter into thy closet, and when thou hast shut thy door, pray to thy Father which is in secret; and thy Father which seeth in secret shall reward thee openly.

But when ye pray, use not vain repetitions, as the heathen do: for they think that they shall be heard for their much speaking.

Be not ye therefore like unto them: for your Father knoweth what things ye have need of, before ye ask him.

After this manner therefore pray ye: Our Father which art in heaven, Hallowed be thy name.

Thy kingdom come, Thy will be done in earth, as it is in heaven.

Give us this day our daily bread.

And forgive us our debts, as we forgive our debtors.

And lead us not into temptation, but deliver us from evil: For thine is the kingdom, and the power, and the glory, for ever. Amen.

For if ye forgive men their trespasses, your heavenly Father will also forgive you:

But if ye forgive not men their trespasses, neither will your Father forgive your trespasses.

Mathew 6:5-15

WHAT ARE COVENANT KEYS TO ANSWERED PRAYER?

And when thou prayest, thou shalt not be as the hypocrites are: for they love to pray standing in the synagogues and in the corners of the streets, that they may be seen of men. Verily I say unto you, They have their reward.
Matthew 6:5

Every time we pray to show off to men that we are praying, we make ourselves hypocrites. If we are to get results in prayer, we must do it privately, from a humbled spirit and from the heart.

Some of us have been praying for decades, yet without concrete results to show for it. Almost everybody is calling on God in prayer every day, without genuine result to prove it. So many of us claim to be men/women of prayer—but God does not hear their prayers. *"Then shall they call upon me, but I will not answer; they shall seek me early, but they shall not find me."* (Proverbs 1:28)

Covenant keys to prayer means: our ability to access heavenly treasures in the realms of the spirit. It literally means our ability to access supernatural treasures through persistent prayers. This includes praying without ceasing, praying in faith, praying boldly, praying from the heart with hope and understanding. By this I mean praying from an expectant heart. If we must receive anything in prayer we must pray believing. *"Be not afraid, only believe."* (Mark 5:36) *"Jesus saith unto them, Believe ye that I am able to do this? They said unto him, Yea, Lord."* (Mathew 9:28)

HIS DESTINY WAS THE CROSS….

HIS PURPOSE WAS LOVE….

HIS REASON WAS YOU….

*And this is the confidence that
we have in him that,
if we ask any thing according to
his will, he heareth us.*

1 John 5:14

THE WINNING PRAYER POINTS

If ye shall ask any thing in my name, I will do it.
John 14:14

—Holy Spirit of God, frustrate and disappoint everyone that is against my life and family, in the name of Jesus.

—Father Lord, destroy every demonic network and trap against my progress in life, in the name of Jesus.

—Fire of God, destroy every demonic projection and curse against my life and destiny, in the name of Jesus.

—Break every spell and curse pronounced against my destiny, in the name of Jesus.

—Hand of God, cage every power militating against my rising in life, in the name of Jesus.

—Power of God, silent every voice raising a counter motion against my elevation, in the name of Jesus.

—Blood of Jesus, neutralize every spirit of Balaam hired to hinder my life, ministry and career, in the name of Jesus.

—Fire of God, break by fire every curse that I have brought into my life through ignorance and disobedience, in the name of Jesus.

—Ancient of day, destroy every power harassing my ministry, in the name of Jesus.

—Father God, deliver me from invincible forces militating against my life and destiny.

—Power of God, frustrate every coven and demonic network, designed to frustrate and hinder my success in life, in the name of Jesus.

—I dismantle every stronghold designed to imprison my talent, in the mighty name of Jesus.

—I reject every cycle of frustration, in the mighty name of Jesus.

—Power of God, paralyze every agent assigned to frustrate my life, in the name of Jesus.

—Finger of God, grant me supernatural speed against all my contenders, in the name of Jesus.

—By the blood of Jesus, I destroy every familiar spirit caging my life and career.

—Fire of God, arrest every demonic agent assigned to police my destiny and marriage.

—By the blood of Jesus, I proclaim no weapon fashioned against me shall ever prosper.

—Holy Spirit of God, break me through and forward in life, in the mighty name of Jesus.

—Mighty God, smash me and renew my strength, in the name of Jesus.

—Holy Spirit, open my eyes to see beyond the visible to the invisible, in the name of Jesus.

—Father Lord, grant me strength and power, in the name of Jesus

—O Lord, liberate my spirit to follow the leading of the Holy Spirit.

—Holy Spirit, teach me to pray through problems instead of praying about them, in the name of Jesus.

—Father Lord, deliver me from the false accusation in life, in the name of Jesus

—By the blood of Jesus, every evil spiritual padlock

and evil chain hindering my success will be roasted, in the name of Jesus.

—By the blood of Jesus, I rebuke every spirit of spiritual deafness and blindness in my life, in the name of the mighty Jesus.

—Father Lord, empower me to dominate the enemy of my destiny, in the name of Jesus.

—Jesus Christ of Nazareth, heal my infirmities, in the name of Jesus

—Lord, anoint my eyes and my ears that they may see and hear wondrous things from heaven.

—Father Lord, anoint me with power and authority to dominate all my enemies, in the name of Jesus.

—Fire of God, roast every giant rising up against my life and career.

—Holy Spirit of God, destroy all my oppressors, in the name of Jesus.

—Angels of good news, bring my good news to me, in the mighty name of Jesus.

—Every strong man holding me down, lose your hold now, in the name of Jesus.

—I nullify every demonic prediction over my life, in the name of Jesus.

—By the blood of Jesus, I flush out every polluted deposit of the enemy in my life.

—By the blood of Jesus, I paralyze every enemy of my promotion, in the name of Jesus.

—Father Lord, destroy any power tormenting my life that is not from You.

—Holy Ghost fire, ignite the fire of revival in my life.

—By the blood of Jesus, I declare victory over every conflicting trial.

—By the blood of Jesus, I command the arrest of every demonic spirit militating against my life.

—By the blood of Jesus, I proclaim the blood of Jesus over every device of the enemy.

—By the blood of Jesus, I revoke stagnation and hardship over my life, in the name of Jesus.

—Holy Ghost fire, destroy every satanic arrangement in my life, in the name of Jesus.

HOW TO PROVOKE
SPIRITUAL BLESSING

And seeing the multitudes, he went up into a mountain:
and when he was set, his disciples came unto him:
And he opened his mouth, and taught them, saying,
Blessed are the poor in spirit:
for theirs is the kingdom of heaven.
Blessed are they that mourn: for they shall be comforted.
Blessed are the meek: for they shall inherit the earth.
Blessed are they which do hunger and thirst
after righteousness: for they shall be filled.
Blessed are the merciful: for they shall obtain mercy.
Blessed are the pure in heart: for they shall see God.
Blessed are the peacemakers:
for they shall be called the children of God.
Blessed are they which are persecuted for righteousness' sake:
for theirs is the kingdom of heaven.
Blessed are ye, when men shall revile you,
and persecute you, and shall say all manner
of evil against you falsely, for my sake.
Rejoice, and be exceeding glad:
for great is your reward in heaven:
for so persecuted they the prophets which were before you.
Matthew 5:1-12

THE LAW OF RECEIVING IS HIDDEN IN GIVING

"To give we must love."

*"For God so loved the world that
he gave his only begotten Son,
that whosoever believeth in him should not perish,
but have everlasting life."*

"To receive, we must give."

It is written, *"Give, and it shall be given unto you; good measure, pressed down, and shaken together, and running over, shall men give into your bosom. For with the same measure that ye mete withal it shall be measured to you again."* (Luke 6:38)

If we must receive in life, we must become givers ourselves. Jesus said it is more of a blessing to give than to receive. Every time we give, we position our life for power and for next level. *"But as many as received him, to them gave he power to become the sons of God, even to them that believe on his name."* (John 1:12)

HOW DO I GIVE?

1) We give cheerfully to God. (2 Corinthians 9:7)

2) We give willingly to God. (1 Corinthians 9:17, Exodus 35:5-22)

3) We give righteously to God. (Malachai 3:3)

4) We give in faith to God. (Ecclesiastes 11:1)

5) We give in love to God. (1 King 3:3, John 3:16)

6) We give liberally to God. (Proverbs 11:25, Proverb 28:27)

7) We give to God for health and longlife. (Psalms 41:1-3, Psalms 91:16)

8) We give to support the kingdom of God. (Matthew 6:33)

9) We give our best, not left over. (Malachai 1:6-8, 2 Samuel 24:24, Genesis 8:20)

CHAPTER 1

How Do I Pray?

But thou, when thou prayest, enter into thy closet, and when thou hast shut thy door, pray to thy Father which is in secret; and thy Father which seeth in secret shall reward thee openly.
Matthew 6:6

If we are to pray correctly, we must follow the footprints of our master Jesus Christ. It is believed that during the Earthy ministry of Jesus Christ, He prayed longer in private—but shorter in public. For us to understand how we should pray, we must start by developing a love for praying without ceasing. We must be disciplined, dedicated and devoted to prayer if we are to witness any tangible results in life. A life full of prayer is no cheap talk. At one point, Jesus prayed so hard that the Bible says his face changed.

And as he prayed, the fashion of his countenance was altered, and his raiment was white and glistering.
Luke 9:28

IN PRIVATE, WE MUST PRAY LONGER AND HUMBLED.
Preferably, kneeling down to pray is a signal

that we are calling on higher power. Our God is bigger than us, so we must remain small in his eyes. Every time we kneel down to pray, we provoke humility. Every time we kneel down to pray, we literally humble ourselves. The posture of kneeling down to pray is a deliberate presentation of humility before God.

Jesus Prayed Kneeling Down

And he was withdrawn from them about a stone's cast, and kneeled down, and prayed.
Luke 22:41

Peter Prayed Kneeling Down

But Peter put them all forth, and kneeled down, and prayed; and turning him to the body said, Tabitha, arise. And she opened her eyes: and when she saw Peter, she sat up.
Acts 9:40

Daniel Kneeled Down to Pray

Now when Daniel knew that the writing was signed, he went into his house; and his windows being open in his chamber toward Jerusalem, he kneeled upon his knees three times a day, and prayed, and gave thanks before his God, as he did aforetime.
Daniel 6:10

Apostle Prayed Kneeling Down

And when he had thus spoken, he kneeled down, and prayed with them all.
Acts 20:36

For the most part, we must present ourselves humbled and kneel down in our private prayer moments with God. Whenever we pray kneeling down, it is a signal that we have respect and honor for our God. God always seeks a humble and meek person to respond to them.

If my people, which are called by my name, shall humble themselves, and pray, and seek my face, and turn from their wicked ways; then will I hear from heaven, and will forgive their sin, and will heal their land.
2 Chronicles 7:14

JESUS GENERATED POWER EVERY TIME HE PRAYED

And as he prayed, the fashion of his countenance was altered, and his raiment was white and glistering.
Luke 9:29

JESUS PROVOKED ANGELIC MINISTRATION THROUGH PRAYERS

And he was there in the wilderness forty days, tempted of Satan; and was with the wild beasts; and the angels ministered unto him.
Mark 1:13

JESUS RECEIVED ANGELIC STRENGTH THROUGH PRAYERS

And there appeared an angel unto him from heaven, strengthening him.
Luke 22:43

HOW DID JESUS TEACH HIS DISCIPLES TO PRAY?

And it came to pass, that, as he was praying in a certain place, when he ceased, one of his disciples said unto him, Lord, teach us to pray, as John also taught his disciples. And he said unto them, When ye pray, say, Our Father which art in heaven, Hallowed be thy name. Thy kingdom come. Thy will be done, as in heaven, so in earth. Give us day by day our daily bread. And forgive us our sins; for we also forgive every one that is indebted to us. And lead us not into temptation; but deliver us from evil.
Luke 11:1-4

WE MUST BE HUMBLED IN PRAYERS

...Thou hast heard the desire of the humble.
Psalms 10:17

If we are to pray with intention to get results, we must be humbled. God hates the proud and arrogant. *"Every one that is proud in heart is an abomination to the Lord."* (Proverbs 16:5) If we are to ask correctly. we must stay away from these things that God hates. *"These six things doth the Lord hate: yea, seven are an abomination unto him: A proud look, a lying tongue, and hands that shed innocent blood, An heart that deviseth wicked imaginations, feet that be swift in running to mischief, A false witness that speaketh lies, and he that soweth discord among brethren."* (Proverbs 6:16)
Remember...

*If my people, which are called by my name,
shall humble themselves, and pray,
and seek my face, and turn from their wicked ways;
then will I hear from heaven,
and will forgive their sin, and will heal their land.*
2 Chronicles 7:14

WE MUST BE RIGHTEOUS

*"The righteous cry, and the Lord heareth,
and delivereth them out of all their troubles."*

Abraham made this profound statement during his prayer encounter with God. *"And Abraham drew near, and said, Wilt thou also destroy the righteous with the wicked? Peradventure there be fifty righteous within the city: wilt thou also destroy and not spare the place for the fifty righteous that are therein? That be far from thee to do after this manner, to slay the righteous with the wicked: and that the righteous should be as the wicked that be far from thee: Shall not the Judge of all the earth do right?"* (Genesis 18:23-25)

A careful examination of the life of Abraham proves to us that God answered Abraham because he was a righteous man. Our God is a righteous God who desires us to be righteous in life also. *"And he believed in the Lord; and he counted it to him for righteousness."* (Genesis 15:6)

HOW DO WE PRAY?

WE MUST PRAY IN FAITH

And the prayer of faith shall save the sick, and the Lord shall raise him up; and if he have committed sins, they shall be forgiven him.
James 5:15

WE MUST PRAY IN THE HOLY GHOST

But ye beloved, building up your selves on your most holy faith, praying in the Holy Ghost.
Jude 1:20

Every time we pray in the Holy Ghost, the Spirit makes intercession for us. The Bible says likewise the Spirit also helpeth our infirmities—for we know not what we should pray for. But the Spirit itself maketh intercession for us with groaning which cannot be uttered. We must begin by asking God in prayers. If we must receive anything in prayer, we must first ask God in prayers. *"... Yet ye have not, because ye ask not."* (James 4:2)

Ask, and it shall be given you; seek, and ye shall find; knock, and it shall be opened unto you: For every one that asketh receiveth; and he that seeketh findeth; and to him that knocketh it shall be opened.
Matthew 7:7-8

If ye then, being evil, know how to give good gifts unto your children, how much more shall your Father which is in heaven give good things to them that ask him?
Matthew 7:11

God is more than willing to answer us because He is a righteous God. God takes pleasure in our breakthroughs, promotion, joy, and happiness in life. *"Let the Lord be magnified, which hath pleasure in the prosperity of his servant."* (Psalms 35:27)

WE MUST PRAY IN FAITH

*By stretching forth thine hand to heal;
and that signs and wonders may be done
by the name of thy holy child Jesus.*
Acts 4:30

WE MUST PRAY BOLDLY

*Let us therefore come boldly
unto the throne of grace that we may obtain mercy,
and find grace to help in time of need.*
Hebrews 4:16

WE MUST PRAY FROM THE HEART

We must pray from the heart. We must engage our spirit every time we pray to God. God does look like man. *"And ye shall seek me, and find me, when ye shall search for me with all your heart."* (Jeremiah 29:13)

GOD LOOKS INTO OUR HEART

A lot of people ask deceivingly not from their heart, but because they just want to consume things they never earned. *"Ye ask, and receive not, because ye ask amiss, that ye may consume it upon your lusts."* (James 4:2-3)

Remember…..

*For the Lord seeth not as man seeth;
for man looketh on the outward appearance,
but the Lord looketh on the heart.*
1 Samuel 16:7

WE MUST PRAY ACCORDING TO THY WILL

*And this is the confidence that we have in him, that,
if we ask any thing according to his will, he heareth us:
And if we know that he hear us, whatsoever we ask, we
know that we have the petitions that we desired of him.*
1 John 5:14-15

WHAT IS THE RIGHT WAY TO PRAY UNTO GOD?

Our case study on how to PRAY is the prayer Jesus taught his disciples to pray in Luke 11:1.

"*And it came to pass, that, as he was praying in a certain place, when he ceased, one of his disciples said unto him, Lord, teach us to pray, as John also taught his disciples. And he said unto them, When ye pray, say, Our Father which art in heaven, Hallowed be thy name. Thy kingdom come. Thy will be done, as in heaven, so in earth. Give us day by day our daily bread. And forgive us our sins; for we also forgive every one that is indebted to us. And lead us not into temptation; but deliver us from evil.*" (Luke 11:1-4)

WE MUST REPENT OF OUR SINS

*Then Peter said unto them, Repent,
and be baptized every one of you
in the name of Jesus Christ for the remission of sins, and
ye shall receive the gift of the Holy Ghost.*
Acts 2:38

WE MUST CONFESS OUR SINS BEFORE HIM

*If we confess our sins, he is faithful and just to forgive
us our sins, and to cleanse us from all unrighteousness.*
1 John 1:9

WE MUST CONFESS OUR SINS BEFORE HIM

*If we confess our sins, he is faithful and just to forgive
us our sins, and to cleanse us from all unrighteousness.*
1 John 1:9

WE MUST PRAY WITH RESPECT

*...The Lord saith, Be it far from me;
for them that honour me I will honour,
and they that despise me shall be lightly esteemed.*
1 Samuel 2:30

WE MUST PRAY WITH REVERENCE TO HIS NAME

*He sent redemption unto his people:
he hath commanded his covenant for ever:
holy and reverend is his name.*
Psalms 111:9

WE MUST HONOR GOD IN PRAYER

A son honoureth his father, and a servant his master: if then I be a father, where is mine honour? and if I be a master, where is my fear? saith the Lord of hosts unto you, O priests, that despise my name. And ye say, Wherein have we despised thy name.
Malachai 1:6

WHEN & HOW OFTEN SHOULD WE PRAY?

ALWAYS!

By this I mean praying as a ritual—without ceasing—throughout life. We are instructed to PRAY ALWAYS. *"Praying always with all prayer and supplication in the Spirit, and watching thereunto with all perseverance and supplication for all saints."* (Ephesians 6:18)

*I thank my God upon every remembrance of you,
Always in every prayer of mine
for you all making request with joy.*
Phillipians 1:3-4

We must PRAY ALWAYS.

We give thanks to God and the Father of our Lord Jesus Christ, praying always for you.
Colossians 1:3

The covenant key to access our treasure is to persevere in ceaseless prayers. This implies praying without ceasing to put the devil far from attacking our lives. *"Pray without ceasing."* (1 Thessalonians 5:17)

Every time we pray and faint or lapse, we lose the battle. We must always keep in mind that prayer is a warfare. If we are to skillfully remain relevant before God, we must embrace ceaseless prayers continually. *"But we will give ourselves continually to prayer, and to the ministry of the word."* Every time we faint, we miss our destined blessing. *"And let us not be weary in well doing: for in due season we shall reap, if we faint not."* (Galatians 6:9)

We must repent, confess and accept the Lord Jesus as our savior.

The Word says as many as received him, to them gave He power to become the sons of God. Even to them that believe on His name.

1) Acknowledge that we are a sinner and that He died for you. (Romans 3:23)

2) Repent of our sins. (Acts 3:19, Luke 13:5, 2 Peter 3:9)

3) Believe in our heart that Jesus died for your sin. (Romans 10:10)

4) Confess Jesus as the Lord over our life. (Romans 10:10, Acts 2:21)

Now repeat this prayer after me:

"Say Lord Jesus, I accept you today, as my Lord and my savior, forgive me of my sins wash me with your blood. Right now, I believe, I am sanctified, I am save, I am free, I am free from the Power of sin to serve the Lord Jesus. Thank you Lord for saving me. Amen."

Congratulations.

YOU ARE NOW A BORN AGAIN CHRISTIAN!

SUMMARY OF CHAPTER ONE

Covenant prayer is a ritual that demands discipline and dedication. If we are to provoke the mysteries of God, we must be determined, devoted and disciplined to engage our hands in battles. *"He teacheth my hands to war, so that a bow of steel is broken by mine arms."* (Pslams 18:34) We must embrace the lifestyle of praying without ceasing. We must go before God, humbled in prayer. We must develop a prayer life. We must embrace praying more in private—but less in public.

And it came to pass, that, as he was praying in a certain place, when he ceased, one of his disciples said unto him, Lord, teach us to pray, as John also taught his disciples. And he said unto them, When ye pray, say, Our Father which art in heaven, Hallowed be thy name. Thy kingdom come. Thy will be done, as in heaven, so in earth. Give us day by day our daily bread. And forgive us our sins; for we also forgive every one that is indebted to us. And lead us not into temptation; but deliver us from evil.
Luke 11:1-4

For us to pray correctly, we must exemplify our prayer from the above teaching of Jesus Christ. We must always ask. Unless we ask, we will not have anything in life.

Remember.....

Ask, and it shall be given you; seek, and ye shall find; knock, and it shall be opened unto you: For every one that asketh receiveth; and he that seeketh findeth; and to him that knocketh it shall be opened.
Matthew 7:7-8

DECISION KEYS

1) Nothing changes until you make up your mind.

2) Decision is the gateway to deliverance.

3) Until you decide, no one will decide for you.

4) Your prosperity is proportional to your decisions.

5) The decision you make will determine the future you will create

6) Decision creates future and fulfills destinies.

7) Decision beautifies our future.

8) Decision keeps you out of trouble.

9) Decision exempts you from evil.

10) Decision gurantees eternity.

11) You can only go far in life by your faith decisions.

12) You are poor because you made such decisions

13) Make a decision and change your life.

14) Life changing decisions are a function of quality information.

15) Success in life is a function of decision.

16) Life experiences are full of decisions.

17) Decisions change destinies.

18) Never settle for information—always look for revelation.

19) You are where you are today based on your last decision.

20) Information is crucial in decision making.

21) Decision makers rule the world.

22) You can rule your world with quality decisions.

23) As long as you decide righteously, Satan cannot harrass you.

CHAPTER 2

THE PRAYER THAT WORKS

But thou, when thou prayest, enter into thy closet, and when thou hast shut thy door, pray to thy Father which is in secret; and thy Father which seeth in secret shall reward thee openly.
Matthew 6:6

Every prayer from the wrong perspective will not work. I believe strongly that there is a prayer that works for us in life. Almost everybody is praying. But whose prayer is generating heaven attention? A blind man who could not see cried, but arrested the attention of Jesus.

"*And when he heard that it was Jesus of Nazareth, he began to cry out, and say, Jesus, thou son of David, have mercy on me. And many charged him that he should hold his peace: but he cried the more a great deal, Thou son of David, have mercy on me. And Jesus stood still, and commanded him to be called. And they call the blind man, saying unto him, Be of good comfort, rise; he calleth thee.*" (Mark 10:47-49)

For our prayer to work, we must do the works of Abraham.

WHAT DO I MEAN BY THE WORKS OF ABRAHAM?

We must have faith in God. With reference to the works of Abraham, it is written: *"He staggered not at the promise of God through unbelief; but was strong in faith, giving glory to God; And being fully persuaded that, what he had promised, he was able also to perform. And therefore it was imputed to him for righteousness."* (Romans 4:20-22)

As a result of our spiritual roots (faith in God), in the Abrahamic covenant our prayer must generate tangible, undeniable results—unless we are yet not saved. *"God heareth not sinners."* (John 9:31)

We must be encouraged to continue to pray to God ceaselessly. It is written, *"Hope deferred maketh the heart sick: but when the desire cometh, it is a tree of life."* (Proverbs 13:12)

We must ceaselessly pray to the God of hope who will prove Himself mighty by answering us speedily. *"Now the God of hope fill you with all joy and peace in believing, that ye may abound in hope, through the power of the Holy Ghost."* (Romans 15:13)

Remember...

> *And this is the confidence that we have in him, that, if we ask any thing according to his will, he heareth us.*
> **1 John 5:14**

What is the prayer that works?

Every heartfelt prayer is acceptable before God. Every prayer from the heart is recorded in heaven. I believe strongly in prayer that works. Frankly, not every prayer works. Some people scream and shout in prayer. Angelic host of heaven finds this very offensive, and I also find this quite offensive. We must all embrace praying from the heart to please Father God. The amplified Bible defines the prayer that works this way:

The heartfelt and persistent prayer of
a righteous man (believer) can accomplish much
when put into action and made effective by God—
it is dynamic and can have tremendous power.
James 5:16

Biblical examples of those who offered heartfelt prayer:

HANNA

And she was in bitterness of soul, and prayed unto the Lord, and wept sore. And she vowed a vow, and said, O Lord of hosts, if thou wilt indeed look on the affliction of thine handmaid, and remember me, and not forget thine handmaid, but wilt give unto thine handmaid a man child, then I will give him unto the Lord all the days of his life, and there shall no razor come upon his head. And it came to pass, as she continued praying before the Lord, that Eli marked her mouth.
1Samuel 1:1:10-12

HEZEKIAH

In those days was Hezekiah sick unto death. And Isaiah the prophet the son of Amoz came unto him, and said unto him, Thus saith the Lord, Set thine house in order: for thou shalt die, and not live. Then Hezekiah turned his face toward the wall, and prayed unto the Lord, And said, Remember now, O Lord, I beseech thee, how I have walked before thee in truth and with a perfect heart, and have done that which is good in thy sight. And Hezekiah wept sore.
Isaiah 38:1-3

JONAH

Then Jonah prayed unto the Lord his God out of the fish's belly, And said, I cried by reason of mine affliction unto the Lord, and he heard me; out of the belly of hell cried I, and thou heardest my voice.
Jonah 2:1-2

WE MUST PRAY KINGDOM ORIENTED PRAYERS

We shall never prevail in prayers unless we focus on the kingdom of GOD. *"But seek ye first the kingdom of God, and his righteousness; and all these things shall be added unto you."* (Matthew 6:33) And he said unto them, When ye pray, say, *"Our Father which art in heaven, Hallowed be thy name. Thy kingdom come. Thy will be done, as in heaven, so in Earth."*

One of my mentors used to say it this way...

"Go after the commission in prayers and the commission will bring the addition in our lives."
~Archbishop Benson Idahosa

CONDITIONS TO RECEIVE THE HOLY SPIRIT

REPENTANCE
"Repent, and be baptized every one of you in the name of Jesus Christ for the remission of sins, and ye shall receive the gift of the Holy Ghost." (Acts 2:38)

BE BAPTIZED
"...be baptized every one of you in the name of Jesus Christ for the remission of sins, and ye shall receive the gift of the Holy Ghost." (Acts 2:38)

CONFESS OF YOUR SIN
"If we confess our sins, he is faithful and just to forgive us our sins, and to cleanse us from all unrighteousness." (1 John 1:9)

ACKNOWLEDGMENT
"Acknowledge that you are a sinner and that Jesus Christ died for your sins." (Romans 3:23)

BORN AGAIN
"Jesus answered and said unto him, Verily, verily, I say unto thee, Except a man be born again, he cannot see the kingdom of God." (John 3:3)

CONDITIONS FOR THE ACQUINTANCE OF THE HOLY SPIRIT

WALKING IN THE SPIRIT
"This I say then, Walk in the Spirit, and ye shall not fulfil the lust of the flesh." (Galatians 5:17)

FAITH
" We having the same spirit of faith, according as it is written, I believed, and therefore have I spoken; we also believe, and therefore speak." (2 Corinthians 4:13)

WALK IN AGREEMENT
"Can two walk together, except they both agreed?" (Amos 3:3)

WALK IN LOVE
"And we have known and believed the love that God hath to us. God is love; and he that dwelleth in love dwelleth in God, and God in him." (1 John 4:16)

WALK IN TRUTH
"If the Son therefore shall make you free, ye shall be free indeed." (John 8:32)

IN SUMMARY
We must pray because prayer is vital for our spiritual growth and nourishment. We must pray if we are to move forward in life. We must pray to see testimonies and speedy answers. We must pray if we

believe in God. I admonish you in the Lord, because prayer works. We all must develop a prayer life for our breakthroughs and promotions, and for our families.

PRAYER POINTS THAT WORK

PRAYER POINT TO PROVOKE COVENANT ANSWERS

—I cancel my name and that of my family's from the death register, with the fire of God, in the mighty name of Jesus.

—Every weapon of destruction fashioned against me and my family be destroyed by the fire of God, in the name of Jesus.

—Power of God, fight for me in every area of my life, in the name of Jesus.

—Every hindrance to my breakthrough be melted by the fire of God, in the name of Jesus.

—Every evil power against me be scattered by the thunder fire of God, in the name of Jesus.

—Father Lord, destroy every evil man/woman, in the name of Jesus.

—Every failure of the past be converted to success, in Jesus' name.

—Father Lord, let the former rain, the latter rain and Your blessing pour down on me now.

—Father Lord, let all the failure turn into success for me, in the name of Jesus.

—I receive power from on high and I paralyze all the

powers of darkness that are diverting my blessings, in the name of Jesus.

—Beginning from this day, I employ the services of the angels of God to open unto me every door of opportunity and breakthroughs, in the name of Jesus.

—I will not go around in circles again, I will make progress, in the name of Jesus.

—I shall not build for another to inhabit and I shall not plant for another to eat, in the name of Jesus.

—I paralyse the powers of the emptier concerning my handiwork, in the name of Jesus.

—O Lord, let every locust, caterpillar and palmer-worm assigned to eat the fruit of my labour be roasted by the fire of God.

—The enemy shall not spoil my testimony in this programme, in the name of Jesus.

—By the blood of Jesus, I reject every backward journey, in the name of Jesus.

—By the blood of Jesus, I paralyze every strongman attached to any area of my life, in the name of Jesus.

—I pray, let every agent of shame fashioned to work against my life be paralyzed, in the name of Jesus.

—I paralyse the activities of household wickedness over my life, in the name of Jesus.

—I quench every strange fire emanating from evil tongues against me, in the name of Jesus.

—Father Lord, give me power for maximum achievement, in the name of Jesus.

—Heavenly Father, give me comforting authority to achieve my goal.

—Blood of Jesus Christ, defend and fortify me with Your power.

—I paralyse every spirit of disobedience in my life, in Jesus' name.

—I refuse to disobey the voice of God, in the name of Jesus.

—Every root of rebellion in my life be uprooted, in Jesus' name.

—By the blood of Jesus, I destroy every witchcraft spirit in my life, in the name of Jesus.

—Perish every contradicting force promoting hindrance in my life, in Jesus' name.

—Every inspiration of witchcraft in my family, be destroyed, in the name of Jesus.

—Blood of Jesus, blot out every evil mark of witchcraft in my life, in the name of Jesus.

—Every garment put upon me by witchcraft, be torn to pieces, in the name of Jesus.

—Angels of God, begin to pursue my household enemies, let their ways be dark and slippery, in the name of Jesus.

—Lord, confuse them and turn them against themselves, in the name of Jesus.

—By the blood of Jesus, I break every evil unconscious agreement with household enemies concerning my miracles, in the name of Jesus.

—Household witchcraft, fall down and die, in the name of Jesus.

—Father Lord, drag all the household wickedness to the Dead Sea and bury them there.

—Father Lord, I refuse to follow the evil pattern of remote control, my household enemies.

—My life, jump out from the cage of household wickedness, in the name of Jesus.

—I command all my blessings and potentials buried by wicked household enemies to be exhumed, in the name of Jesus.

—I will see the goodness of the Lord in the land of the living, in the name of Jesus.

—Everything done against me to spoil my joy receive destruction, in the name of Jesus.

—Father Lord, as Abraham received favour in Your eyes, let me receive Your favour, so that I can excel in every area of my life.

—Lord Jesus, help my shortcomings and infirmities, in the name of Jesus.

—It does not matter whether I deserve it or not, I receive immeasurable favour from the Lord, in the name of Jesus.

—By the blood of Jesus I receive every blessing God has apportioned to me, in the name of Jesus.

—My blessing will not be transferred to my neighbor, in the name of Jesus.

—Father Lord, disgrace every power that is tormenting my breakthrough, in the name of Jesus.

—Every step I take shall lead to outstanding success, in Jesus' name.

—I shall prevail with man and with God in every area of my life, in the name of Jesus.

—Break to pieces every habitation of infirmity in my

life, in the name of Jesus.

—My body, soul and spirit, reject every evil load, in Jesus' name.

—Evil foundation in my life, I pull you down today, in the mighty name of Jesus.

—Every inherited sickness in my life, depart from me now, in the name of Jesus.

—Every evil water in my body, get out, in the name of Jesus.

—By the blood of Jesus, I cancel the effect of every evil dedication in my life, in the name of Jesus.

—Holy Ghost fire, immunize my blood against satanic poisoning, in the name of Jesus.

—Father Lord, put self-control in my mouth, in the name of Jesus.

—I refuse to get accustomed to sickness, in the name of Jesus.

—Every door open to infirmity in my life, be permanently closed today, in the name of Jesus.

—Every power contenting with God in my life, be roasted, in the name of Jesus.

—Every power preventing God's glory from manifesting in my life, be paralysed, in the name of Jesus.

—I loose myself from the spirit of desolation, in the name of Jesus.

—Father Lord, break me through in my home, in the name of Jesus.

—Father Lord keep in me healthy, in the name of Jesus.

—Father Lord break me through in my business, in the

name of Jesus.

—Let God be God in my economy, in the name of Jesus.

—Glory of God, envelope every department of my life, in the name of Jesus.

—The Lord that answereth by fire, be my God, in the name of Jesus.

—By the blood of Jesus, all my enemies shall scatter to rise no more, in the name of Jesus.

—Blood of Jesus, cry against all evil gatherings arranged for my sake, in the name of Jesus.

—Father Lord, convert all my past failures to unlimited victories, in the name of Jesus.

—Lord Jesus, create room for my advancement in every area of my life.

—All evil thoughts against me, Lord turn them to be good for me.

—Father Lord, give evil men for my life where evil decisions have been taken against me, in the name of Jesus.

—Father Lord, advertise Your dumbfounding prosperity in my life.

—Let the showers of dumbfounding prosperity fall in every department of my life, in the name of Jesus.

—By the blood of Jesus, I claim all my prosperity in the name of Jesus.

—Every door of my prosperity that has been shut, be opened now, in the name of Jesus.

—Father Lord, convert my poverty to prosperity, in the name of Jesus.

—Father Lord, convert my mistake to perfection, in the name of Jesus.

—Father Lord, convert my frustration to fulfillment, in the name of Jesus.

—Father Lord, bring honey out of the rock for me, in the name of Jesus.

—By the blood of Jesus, I stand against every evil covenant of sudden death, in the name of Jesus.

—By the blood of Jesus, I break every conscious and unconscious evil covenant of untimely death, in the name of Jesus.

—You spirit of death and hell, you have no document in my life, in the name of Jesus.

—You stones of death, depart from my ways, in the name of Jesus.

—Father Lord, make me a voice of deliverance and blessing.

—By the blood of Jesus, I tread upon the high places of the enemies, in the name of Jesus.

—I bind and render useless, every blood-sucking demon, in the name of Jesus.

—You evil current of death, lose your grip over my life, in the name of Jesus.

—By the blood of Jesus, I frustrate the decisions of the evil openers in my family, in the name of Jesus.

—Fire of protection, cover my family, in the name of Jesus.

—Father Lord, make my way perfect, in the name of Jesus.

—Throughout the days of my life, I shall not be put to

shame, in the name of Jesus.

—By the blood of Jesus, I reject every garment of shame, in the name of Jesus.

—By the blood of Jesus, I reject every shoe of shame, in the name of Jesus.

—By the blood of Jesus, I reject every head-gear and cap of shame, in the name of Jesus.

—Shamefulness shall not be my lot, in the mighty name of Jesus.

—Be removed every demonic limitation of my progress as a result of shame, in the name of Jesus.

—Every network of shame around me be paralysed, in the name of Jesus.

—Those who seek for my shame shall die for my sake, in the name of Jesus.

—As far as shame is concerned, I shall not record any point for satan, in the name of Jesus.

—In the name of Jesus, I shall not eat the bread of sorrow, I shall not eat the bread of shame and I shall not eat the bread of defeat.

—No evil will touch me throughout my life, in the name of Jesus.

—By the blood of Jesus, in every area of my life, my enemies will not catch me, in the name of Jesus.

—By the blood of Jesus, in every area of my life, I shall run and not grow weary, I shall walk and shall not faint.

—Father Lord, in every area of my life, let not my life disgrace You.

—By the blood of Jesus, I will not be a victim of failure and I shall not bite my finger for any reason, in the name of Jesus.

—Holy Spirit of God, help me O Lord, to meet up with God's standard for my life.

—By the blood of Jesus, I refuse to be a candidate to the spirit of amputation, in the name of Jesus.

—By the blood of Jesus, with each day of my life, I shall move to higher ground, in the name of Jesus.

—Every spirit of shame set in motion against my life, I bind you, in the name of Jesus.

—Every spirit competing with my breakthroughs, be chained, in the name of Jesus.

—By the blood of Jesus, I bind every spirit of slavery, in the name of Jesus.

—By the blood of Jesus, in every day of my life, I disgrace all my stubborn pursuers, in the name of Jesus.

—By the blood of Jesus, I bind every spirit of Herod, in the name of Jesus.

—Every spirit challenging my God, be disgraced, in Jesus' name.

—Every Red Sea before me, be parted, in the name of Jesus.

—By the blood of Jesus, I command every spirit of bad-ending to be bound in every area of my life, in the name of Jesus.

—By the blood of Jesus, every spirit of Saul be disgraced in my life, in the name of Jesus.

—By the blood of Jesus, every spirit of Pharaoh be disgraced in my life, in Jesus' name.

—By the blood of Jesus, I reject every evil invitation to

backwardness, in Jesus' name.

—By the blood of Jesus, I command every stone of hindrance in my life to be rolled away, in the name of Jesus.

—Father Lord, roll away every stone of poverty from my life, in the name Jesus.

—Let every stone of infertility in my marriage be rolled away, in the name of Jesus.

—Let every stone of non-achievement in my life be rolled away, in the name of Jesus.

—My God, roll away every stone of hardship and slavery from my life, in the name of Jesus.

—My God, roll away every stone of failure planted in my life, in my home and in my business, in the name of Jesus.

—You stones of hindrance planted at the edge of my breakthroughs, be rolled away, in the name of Jesus.

—You stones of stagnancy stationed at the border of my life, be rolled away, in the name of Jesus.

—My God, let every stone of the 'amputator' planted at the beginning of my life, at the middle of my life and at the end of my life, be rolled away, in the name of Jesus.

—Father Lord, I thank You for all the stones You have rolled away, I forbid their return, in the name of Jesus.

—Let the power from above come upon me, in the name of Jesus.

—Father Lord, advertise Your power in every area of my life, in the name of Jesus.

—Father Lord, make me a power generator throughout the days of my life, in the name of Jesus.

—Let the power to live a holy life throughout the days of my life fall upon me, in the name of Jesus.

—Let the power to live a victorious life throughout the days of my life fall upon me, in the name of Jesus.

—Let the power to prosper throughout the days of my life fall upon me, in the name of Jesus.

—Let the power to be in good health throughout the days of my life fall upon me, in the name of Jesus.

—Let the power to disgrace my enemies throughout the days of my life fall upon me, in the name of Jesus.

—Let the power of Christ rest upon me now, in the name of Jesus.

—Let the power to bind and loosen fall upon me now, in the name of Jesus.

—Father Lord, let Your key of revival unlock every department of my life for Your revival fire, in the name of Jesus.

—Every area of my life that is at the point of death, receive the touch of revival, in the name of Jesus.

—Father Lord, send down Your fire and anointing into my life, in the name of Jesus.

—Every uncrucified area in my life, receive the touch of fire and be crucified, in the name of Jesus.

—Let the fire fall and consume all hindrances to my advancement, in the name of Jesus.

—You stubborn problems in my life, receive the Holy Ghost dynamite, in the name of Jesus.

—You carryover miracle from my past receive the touch of fire, in the name of Jesus.

—Holy Ghost fire, baptize me with prayer miracle, in Jesus' name.

—By the blood of Jesus, every area of my life that needs deliverance, receive the touch of fire and be delivered, in the name of Jesus.

—Let my angels of blessing locate me now, in the name of Jesus.

—Every satanic programme of impossibility, I cancel you now, in the name of Jesus.

—Every household wickedness and its programme of impossibility, be paralysed, in the name of Jesus.

—No curse will land on my head, in the name of Jesus.

—Throughout the days of my life, I will not waste money on my health: the Lord shall be my healer, in the name of Jesus.

—Throughout the days of my life, I will be in the right place at the right time.

—Throughout the days of my life, I will not depart from the fire of God's protection, in the name of Jesus.

—Throughout the days of my life, I will not be a candidate for incurable disease, in the name of Jesus.

—Every weapon of captivity be disgraced, in the name of Jesus.

—Lord, before I finish this programme, I need an outstanding miracle in every area of my life.

—Let every attack planned against the progress of my life be frustrated, in the name of Jesus.

—I command the spirits of harassment and torment to leave me, in the name of Jesus.

—Lord, begin to speak soundness into my mind and

being, in Jesus' name.

—I reverse every witchcraft curse issued against my progress, in the name of Jesus.

—I condemn all the spirits condemning me, in the name of Jesus.

—Let divine accuracy come into my life and operations, in the name of Jesus.

—No evil directive will manifest in my life, in the name of Jesus.

—Let the plans and purposes of heaven be fulfilled in my life, in the name of Jesus.

—O Lord, bring to me friends that reverence Your name and keep all others away.

—Let divine strength come into my life, in the name of Jesus.

—Let every stronghold working against my peace be destroyed, in the name of Jesus.

—Let the power to destroy every decree of darkness operating in my life fall upon me now, in the mighty name of Jesus.

—Lord, deliver my tongue from evil silence.

—Lord, let my tongue tell others of Your life.

—Lord, loosen my tongue and use it for Your glory.

—Lord, let my tongue bring straying sheep back to the fold.

—Lord, let my tongue strengthen those who are discouraged.

—Lord, let my tongue guide the sad and the lonely.

—Lord, baptise my tongue with love and fire.

—Let every unrepentant and stubborn pursuers be disgraced in my life, in the name of Jesus.

—Let every iron-like curse working against my life be broken by the blood of Jesus, in the name of Jesus.

—Let every problem designed to disgrace me receive open shame, in the name of Jesus.

—Let every problem anchor in my life be uprooted, in Jesus' name.

—Multiple evil covenants, be broken by the blood of Jesus, in the name of Jesus.

—Multiple curses, be broken by the blood of Jesus, in
—Jesus' name.

—Everything done against me with evil padlocks, be nullified by the blood of Jesus, in the name of Jesus.

—Everything done against me at any crossroads, be nullified by the blood of Jesus, in the name of Jesus.

—Let every stubborn and prayer resisting demon receive stones of fire and thunder, in the name of Jesus.

—Every stubborn and prayer-resisting sickness, lose your evil hold upon my life, in the name of Jesus.

—Every problem associated with the dead, be smashed by the blood of Jesus, in the name of Jesus.

—I recover my stolen property sevenfold, in the name of Jesus.

—Let every evil memory about me be erased by the blood of Jesus, in the name of Jesus.

—By the blood of Jesus, I disallow my breakthroughs from being caged, in Jesus' name.

—Let the sun of my prosperity arise and scatter every cloud of poverty, in the name of Jesus.

—I decree unstoppable advancement upon my life, in

Jesus' name.

—I soak every day of my life in the blood of Jesus and in signs and wonders, in the name of Jesus.

—I break every stronghold of oppression in my life, in Jesus' name.

—Let every satanic joy about my life be terminated, in the name of Jesus.

—I paralyse every household wickedness, in the name of Jesus.

—Let every satanic spreading river dry up by the blood of Jesus, in the name of Jesus.

—I bind every ancestral spirit and command them to loose their hold over my life, in the name of Jesus.

CHAPTER 3

THE BENEFITS OF PRAYER

Although prayer is our established means of communication with the Father, it is also an avenue for genuine relationship and fellowship with the Holy Spirit. Quite frankly, the benefits of prayer are supernatural. Among a few are the fact that prayer enables you to be focused in life and helps set your mind on the things above. This includes timely direction, deliverance from wrong decisions, eliminating trouble, worry and anxiety, producing and releasing peace and love, provoking fellowship and relationship with the Holy Spirit, granting confidence, making us more sensitive to the ways of the spirit, granting us opportunities and promotion.

If my people, which are called by my name, shall humble themselves, and pray, and seek my face, and turn from their wicked ways; then will I hear from heaven, and will forgive their sin, and will heal their land.
2 Chronicles 7:14

PRAYER MAKES US BOLD
"Let us therefore come boldly unto the throne of grace, that we may obtain mercy, and find grace to help in time of need." (Hebrews 4:16)

PRAYER GRANTS US CONFIDENCE
"And this is the confidence that we have in him that, if we ask any thing according to his will, he heareth us." (1 John 5:14)

PRAYER ALLOWS US TO FELLOWSHIP
"If we confess our sins, he is faithful and just to forgive us our sins, and to cleanse us from all unrighteousness." (1 John 1:9)

PRAYER HUMBLES OUR SPIRIT MAN
"If my people, which are called by my name, shall humble themselves, and pray, and seek my face." (2 Chronicles 7:14)

PRAYER GRANTS US DIVINE DIRECTION
"I will instruct thee and teach thee in the way which thou shalt go: I will guide thee with mine eye." (Psalms 32:8)

PRAYER GRANTS US PROFIT
"I am the Lord thy God which teacheth thee to profit, which leadeth thee by the way that thou shouldest go." (Isaiah 48:17)

PRAYER MAKES US FAITHFUL
"Faithful is he that calleth you, who also will do it." (1 Thessalonians 5:24)

PRAYER MAKES US A BETTER MORAL CITIZEN
The ritual of prayer is a lifestyle that demands us to be righteous, disciplined and determined in life. We become a better moral citizen with a life of prayer

PRAYER DELIVERS US FROM EVIL
We are set free from all the wiles and schemes of the devil—as long as we can pray.

PRAYER IS MEDICINAL
"And the prayer of faith shall save the sick." (James 5:15)

WHEN DAVID PRAYED FOR SOLOMON IS LASTED FOR GENERATIONS YET UNBORN
(See Psalms 72)

PRAYER IS A FAMILY LEGACY
"A good man leaveth an inheritance to his children's children." (Proverbs 13:22)

One great example of the benefit of prayer is Jonathan Edwards, the Puritan preacher from the 1700s. Jonathan and his wife, Sarah, left a great Godly legacy for their 11 children—compared to Max Jukes, who was a drunkard and never prayed in his lifetime. At the beginning of the 20th century, American educator and pastor A.E. Winship decided to trace out the descendants of Jonathan Edwards almost 150 years after his death.

His findings were remarkable, astounding and undeniable—especially when compared to the lifeline Max Jukes. Jukes' legacy became public when the family trees of 42 different men in the New York prison system were traced back to him.

On the other hand, Jonathan Edwards'

PRAYER LEGACY includes: 1 U.S. Vice-President, 3 U.S. Senators, 3 governors, 3 mayors, 13 college presidents, 30 judges, 65 professors, 80 public office holders, 100 lawyers and 100 missionaries. Max Jukes' descendants included: 7 murderers, 60 thieves, 50 women of debauchery, 130 other convicts, 310 paupers (with over 2,300 years lived in poorhouses) and another 400 who were physically wrecked by indulgent living. It was estimated that Max Juke's descendants cost the state more than $1.25 million.

Clearly, a prayer lifestyle has a profound impact on the children of all Godly families who depend on God in prayers.

CONCLUSION

Call unto me, and I will answer thee, and show thee great and mighty things, which thou knowest not.
Jeremiah 33:3

Unless otherwise stated, we must all come unto repentance if we are to encounter our savior Jesus Christ. Repentance is the key to deliverance, protection and promotion. Everyone who desired to encounter testimonies in their prayers must confess and forsake their sinful ways and go after God.

Let us hear the conclusion of the whole matter:
Fear God, and keep his commandments:
for this is the whole duty of man.
For God shall bring every work into judgment,
with every secret thing, whether it be good,
or whether it be evil.
Ecclesiastes 12:13-14

The entire book will remain a story to everyone who is not ready to make a decision for Jesus Christ. A wise man once said, "If we fail to plan, we have planned to fail." We want you to make plans to make heaven. The Bible says in Ecclesiastes 12:14—*"For God shall bring every work into judgment, with every secret thing, whether it be good, or whether it be evil."* If you are a born again Christian we'd like to encourage you in your Christian life. If you are not a born again Christian, we can help you here receive genuine salvation.

Therefore if any man be in Christ,
he is a new creature: old things are passed away;
behold, all things are become new.
2 Corinthians 5:17

WHAT MUST I DO TO DETERMINE MY DIVINE VISITATION?

To determine divine visitation you must be born again!

The Word says as many as received him, to them gave He power to become the sons of God. Even to them that believe on His name. To qualify for divine visitation do the following sincerely:

1) Acknowledge that we are a sinner and that He died for you. (Romans 3:23)

2) Repent of our sins. (Acts 3:19, Luke 13:5, 2 Peter 3:9)

3) Believe in our heart that Jesus died for your sin. (Romans 10:10)

4) Confess Jesus as the Lord over your life. (Romans 10:10, Acts 2:21)

Now repeat this prayer after me:

"Say Lord Jesus, I accept you today, as my Lord and my savior, forgive me of my sins wash me with your blood. Right now, I believe, I am sanctified, I am save, I am free, I am free from the Power of sin to serve the Lord Jesus. Thank you Lord for saving me. Amen."

Congratulations.

YOU ARE NOW A BORN AGAIN CHRISTIAN!

AGAIN I SAY TO YOU...

CONGRATULATIONS!

I adjure you to watch the Spirit of God bearing witness, with your Spirit confirming His word with signs. The Word says the Spirit itself beareth witness with our spirit, that we are the children of God. Join a Bible-believing church—or join us for our weekly and Sunday worship services at 343 Sanford Avenue, Newark, New Jersey 07106.

WISDOM KEYS

—Every productive society is a society heading to the top.

—Millions of Nigerians run away from Nigeria. Very few Nigerians stay in Nigeria.

—My decision to return Nigeria is the will of God for my life.

—My shortcoming in America after 18 years is the fact that I've trained me to be wise, to think, reflect and reason appropriately.

—If you train your mind to reason, it will train your hands to earn money.

—It is absurd to use the money of the heathen to build the kingdom of the living God.

—Every ministry reveals its agenda and VISION either at the beginning or at the end.

—Be careful of your life. It is your first ministry.

—The average American mind is conditioned for a continual quest to get new things and discard the old.

—When I considered well, my BMW jeep became my initial deposit for the work of the ministry in Nigeria.

—Money will never fall from any tree or person. Make up your mind to be independent today.

—Everyone is waiting for you to change your mind. Until you change your thinking, nothing changes around you.

—Multiple academic degrees in other disciplines gave me the chance to think and reason.

—Whatever anyone is thinking at any time reveals what is inside of their heart.

—All planned events are the product of meditation.

—Every event is designed for a designated timeline.

—Wisdom is your ability to think, to create and invent.

— If you can think wisely enough, you will come out of debt.

—The distance between you and your success is your innovative and creative ability to think well.

—Success is the result of hard work, commitment, resolve and determined learning from past mistakes and failings.

—If you organize your mind, you have organized your

life and destiny.

—There is a thin line between success and failure.

—Wealth is your ability to think, power is your ability to reason and success is your ability to be informed.

—If you can make use of your mind by thinking and reasoning, God will make use of your life and destiny.

—Reflect, reason, think and be great.

—Famous people are born of woman.

—That you will make it is your intention, that you will survive is your resolve, that you will succeed with changes is your determination, personal efforts and hard work.

—No man was born a failure.

—Lack of vision is the result of failure.

—Working with mental patients encourages and aspire me to be a productive observant and dedicated to my assignment.

—Successful people are not magicians. It is the will-power, combined with hard work and determination and a resolve to succeed, that make them succeed.

—In the unequivocal state of the mind, intention is not a location or a position. It is the state of the mind.

—So many people think that they think. The mind is used to think, to reflect and to reason. You will remain blind with your eyes open until you can see with your mind by thinking.

—There is no favoritism in accurate and precise calculation.

—Although knowledge is power, information is the key and gateway to a great future.

—It will take the hand of God to move the hand of man.

—With the backing of the great wise God, nothing will disconnect you from your inheritance.

—As long as you have wisdom and understanding of God, Satan and evil cannot manipulate your life and destiny.

—You have come this far in life by your own judgment and the decisions you made in the past. Now lean in and listen to God for another dimension of greatness.

—Great people are ordinary people. It is extra ordinary efforts and the price of sacrifice that produces greatness in them.

—As a mental direct care worker, I saw a great pastor and a motivational speaker within myself.

—A menial job does not reduce your self-worth. Until you resolve to achieve greatness and see greatness in all you do, you will never count in your community.

—The principle of Jesus will solve your gambling and addiction problems.

—The man of Jesus will lead you into heaven.

—Everyone has their self-appraisal and what they think about you. Until you discover yourself, other opinions about you will alter the real you.

—Supervisors and directors are just a position in the chain of command in a workplace. Never allow your supervisor hierarchy to alter your opinion of yourself.

—Everyone can come out of debt if they make up their mind.

—The fact that I am not a decision-maker at work does not diminish my contribution to my world.

—Although it appears like it was a poor decision to accept a direct care employment at a psychiatric hospital, as I reflect on my nine years of that experience, it became apparent that I have learned and experienced enough for my next assignment.

—Self-encouragement and determination is a resolve of the heart.

—If you are determined to make a difference and do the things that make a difference, you will eventually make a difference.

—Good things do not come easy.

—Short cuts will cut your life short.

—Those who look ahead move ahead.

—Life is all about making an impact. In your lifetime strive to make an impact in your community.

—Make friends and connect with people who are moving ahead of you in life.

—If you can look around well, you have come a long way in your life, made a lot of difference and realized a lot of success in life.

—If you are my old friend, hurry up to reach out to me before I become a stranger to you.

—I am blessed with inspirations from God that changed my interpretation of the world around me.

—I thought I was stagnant and lonely until I looked around and noticed my children running around and my wife cooking.

—At 40, I resigned my job to seek the Lord forever.

—My ministry took a drastic rise to the top when the wisdom of God visited me with knowledge and understanding.

—You will be a better person if you understand the characteristics of your personality like your mood swings, attitudes and habits.

—It is the seed of love you sow into the heart of a child and a woman that you reap in due time.

—Love is not selfish. Love shares everything, including the concealed secrets of the mind.

—As long as you have a prayer life and a Bible, you will never feel lonely in the race of life.

—When good friends disconnect from you, let them go. They might have seen something new in a different direction.

—Confidence in yourself and in God is the only way to bring you out of captivity

—Never train a child to waste his or her time.

—The mind is the greatest asset of a great future.

—You walk by common sense, run by principles and fly by instruction.

—Those who become successful in life did it by self-determination, hard work and learning from past failures.

—Most successful people are lonely people. No one renders help to them, believing they are already successful. Except when they seek for more knowledge and information, they are all alone.

— I have seen a towing truck vehicle. I have also seen a towing ship in the water. But I have never seen a towing airplane in the air.

—I exercise my judgment and make a decision every minute of the day. Decisions are crucial, critical and vital with reference to your future.

—So many people wish for a great future. You can only work towards a great future.

—Your celebrity status began when you discovered

your talent. What are you good at? Work at it with all your commitment.

—Prayers will sustain you, but the wisdom of God will prosper you.

—When I met Oyedepo, his teachings changed my perspective. But when I met Ibiyeomie, his teachings changed my perception.

—I will be successful in ministry if only I concentrate and focus my energy in the work of the ministry.

—It took the late Dr. Norman Vincent Peale's book to open my mind towards the kingdom of success.

CHAPTER 4

PRAYER OF SALVATION

*Neither is there salvation in any other:
for there is none other name under heaven
given among men, whereby we must be saved.*
Acts 4:12

What must I do to determine my divine visitation?

To be saved, we must be born again!

The word says, *"As many as received Him, to them gave He power to become the sons of God. Even to them that believe on his name."* (John 1:12)

To qualify for divine visitation, do the following with sincerity—

1) Acknowledge that you are a sinner and that He died for you. (Romans 3:23)

2) Repent of your sins. (Acts 3:19, Luke 13:5, 2 Peter 3:9)

3) Believe in your heart that Jesus died for your sins. (Romans 10:10)

4) Confess Jesus as the Lord over your life.
(Romans 10:10, Acts 2:21)

Now repeat this prayer after me:

Say Lord Jesus, I accept you today, as my Lord and my savior. Forgive me of my sins, wash me with your blood. Right now, I believe I am sanctified, I am saved, I am free. I am free from the power of sin, to serve the Lord Jesus. Thank you Lord for saving me. Amen.

Congratulations. You are now...

A BORN AGAIN CHRISTIAN.

Again I say to you—CONGRATULATIONS!

I adjure you to watch the Spirit of God bear witness with your Spirit, confirming His word with subsequent signs. The word says, *"The Spirit itself beareth witness with our spirit, that we are the children of God."* (Romans 8:16)

MIRACLE CARE OUTREACH

"...But that the members should have the same care one for another"
1 Corinthians 12:25

We are all members of the body of Christ. Jesus commanded us to love our neighbor as ourselves. This includes caring for one another as a member of one body. True love is expressed in caring and giving. The word says, for God so Love He gave....

Reach out to someone in need of Jesus. Help someone in crisis find Christ. Look out and prove your love to Jesus by caring and inviting your friends and associates to find Jesus the Healer.

Invite your friends to our Home Care Cell Fellowship (Miracle Chapel Intl. Satellite Fellowship). We're in the U.S. at 33 Schley Street, Newark, New Jersey 07112. Home Care Cell Fellowship Group meets every Tuesday at 6:00pm-7:00pm.

If you are in Nigeria—MIRACLE OF GOD MINISTRIES, aka "MIRACLE CHAPEL INTL." Mpama–Egbu-Owerri Imo state Nigeria.

LIFE IS NOT ALL ABOUT DURATION, BUT IT'S ALL ABOUT DONATION

What does this statement mean?

Life consists not in accumulation of material wealth. (Luke 12:15) But it's all about liberality…i.e., what you can give and share with others. (Proverbs 11:25) When you live for others, you live forever—because you outlive your generation by the legacy you leave behind after you depart into glory to be with the Lord. But when you live for yourself, when you are reduced to self—you are easily forgotten when you die and depart in glory.

Permit me to admonish you today to live your life to be a blessing to a soul connected to you today. I want you to know that so many souls are connected and looking up to you, and through you so many souls will be saved and rescued from destruction. Will you disciple someone today to find Jesus Christ?

As a genuine Christian, it is your duty to evangelize Jesus Christ to all you meet on your way. Jesus is still in the healing business—Jesus is still doing miracles, from time of old to now. Therefore, tell someone about Jesus Christ today, disciple and bring them to Church. *Philip findeth Nathanael…* (John 1:45)

Please prove the sincerity of your love for God today, please become a soul winner. The dignity of your Christianity is hidden in your boldness to proclaim and evangelize Jesus Christ to all you meet on your way. There is a question mark on the integrity of your Christianity until you become a life soul winner. Invite someone to join us worship the Lord Jesus this coming Sunday. Amen.

MIRACLE OF GOD MINISTRIES

PILLARS OF THE COMMISSION

We Believe, Preach and Practice the following:

1) We believe and preach Salvation to every living human being.

2) We believe and preach Repentance and Forgiveness of sins.

3) We believe and preach the baptism of the Holy Spirit and Spiritual gifts.

4) We believe and teach Prosperity.

5) We believe and preach Divine Healing and Miracles—Signs and Wonder.

6) We believe and preach Faith.

7) We believe and proclaim the Power of God (Supernatural).

8) We believe and proclaim Praise and Worship to God.

9) We believe and preach Wisdom.

10) We believe and preach Holiness (Consecration).

11) We believe and preach Vision.

12) We believe and teach the Word of God.

13) We believe and teach Success.

14) We believe and practice Prayer.

15) We believe and teach Deliverance.

These 15 stones form the Pillars of Our Commission.
Become part of this church family and follow this great move of God.

MY HEARTFELT PRAYER FOR YOU

It is my prayer that you testify today about the goodness of the Lord. I desire for you to have an encounter with our Lord Jesus Christ.

Now let me pray for you:

Heavenly father may today be a day of new beginning for this precious love one. Lord God of heaven open a new chapter in the life of this precious love one reading this book today. May all their secret prayers be answered in the mighty name of Jesus. We thank you Jesus for hearing us. In Jesus mighty name. Amen.

WHAT TO DO WHEN MIRACLES SEEM TO BE DELAYED

1. Praise God even in times of trouble, trial and tribulations.

2. Be expectant—expect God to move beyond imagination.

3) Be willing and obedient—God look at your obedient in times of delay.

4) Be focused—God expects us to pay relevant attention to details.

5) Do not quit—If we must emerge winners, quitting is not an option.

6) Be positive—it can only get better, so be positive.

7) Be optimistic—your case is different so be optimistic in life.

8) Develop an all possibility mentality—every limitation is within your faith.

*****TIME TO TURN TO GOD*****

Have you ever asked why are you here?

God planted you here to bring to pass his counsel and plan over your life.

The best of your physical strengths and efforts are the beginning of God's grace.

Eternity is real. Heaven is sure. Become interested in the heavenly race and book your name in the lamb book of life.

Everything great comes by His grace upon your life.

Therefore, turn unto God in suplication—in thanksgiving and in prayer—and God will surely turn in your favor.

CHAPTER 5

ABOUT THE AUTHOR

Rev. Franklin N. Abazie is the founding and Presiding Pastor of Miracle of God Ministries, with headquarters in Newark, New Jersey USA and a branch church in Owerri-Imo State Nigeria. He is following the footsteps of one of his mentors, the healing evangelist Oral Roberts of the blessed memory. The Lord passed Oral Roberts' healing mantle two days before he went to be with the Lord at age 91 into the hands of healing evangelist Rev. Franklin N. Abazie in a vision.

In all his services, the Power and Presence of God is present to heal all in his audience. Rev. Abazie is an ordained man of God, with a Healing Ministry reviving the healing and miracle ministry of Jesus Christ of Nazareth.

Pastor Franklin N. Abazie, has been called by God with a unique mandate: **"THE MOMENT IS DUE TO IMPACT YOUR WORLD THROUGH THE REVIVAL OF THE HEALING AND MIRACLE MINISTRY OF JESUS CHRIST OF NAZARETH.**

"I AM SENDING YOU TO RESTORE HEALTH UNTO THEE AND I WILL HEAL THEE OF THY WOUNDS, SAID THE LORD OF HOST."

Chapter 5   About the Author

Rev. Abazie is a gifted, ardent teacher of the word of God, who operates also in the office of a Prophet, generating and attracting undeniable signs and wonders, special miracles and healings, with apostolic fireworks of the Holy Ghost. He is the founding and presiding senior Pastor of this fast growing Healing Ministry. He has written over 86 inspirational, healing and transforming books covering almost all aspects of divine healing and life. He is happily married and blessed with children.

BOOKS BY REV. FRANKLIN N. ABAZIE:

1) The Outcome of Faith
2) Understanding the Secret of Prevailing Prayers
3) Commanding Abundance
4) Understanding the Secret of the Man God Uses
5) Activating My Due Season
6) Overcoming Divine Verdicts
7) The Outcome of Divine Wisdom
8) Understanding God's Restoration Mandate
9) Walking In the Victory and Authority of the Truth
10) God's Covenant Exemption
11) Destiny Restoration Pillars
12) Provoking Acceptable Praise
13) Understanding Divine Judgment
14) Activating Angelic Re-enforcement
15) Provoking Un-Merited Favo
16) The Benefits of the Speaking Faith
17) Understanding Divine Arrangement
18) How to Keep Your Healing
19) Understanding the Mysteries of the Speaking Faith
20) Understanding the Mysteries of Prophetic Healing
21) Operating Under the Rules of Creative Healing
22) Understanding the Joy of Breakthrough
23) Understanding the Mystery of Breakthrough
24) Understanding Divine Prosperity
25) Understanding Divine Healing
26) Retaining Your Inheritance
27) Overcoming Confusing Spirit
28) Commanding Angelic Escorts

29) Enforcing Your Inheritance In Christ Jesus
30) Understanding Your Guardian Angels
31) Overcoming the Dominion of Sin
32) Understanding the Voice of God
33) The Outstanding Benefits of the Anointing
34) The Audacity of the Blood of Jesus
35) Walking in the Reality of the Anointing
36) Escaping the Nightmare of Poverty
37) Understanding Your Harvest Season
38) Activating Your Success Buttons
39) Overcoming the Forces of Darkness
40) Overcoming the Devices of the Devil
41) Overcoming Demonic Agents
42) Overcoming the Sorrows of Failure
43) Rejecting the Sorrows of Failure
44) Resisting the Sorrows of Poverty
45) Restoring Broken Marriages
46) Redeeming Your Days
47) The Force of Vision
48) Overcoming the Forces of Ignorance
49) Understanding the Sacrifice of Small Beginning
50) The Might of Small Beginning
51) Understanding the Mysteries of Prophesy
52) Overcoming Dream Nightmares
53) Breaking the Shackles of the Curse of the Law
54) Understanding the Joy of Harvest
55) Wisdom for Signs & Wonders
56) Wisdom for Generational Impact
57) Wisdom for Marriage Stability
58) Understanding the Number of Your Days

59) Enforcing Your Kingdom Rights
60) Escaping the Traps of Immoralities
61) Escaping the Trap of Poverty
62) Accessing Biblical Prosperity
63) Accessing True Riches in Christ
64) Silencing the Voice of the Accuser
65) Overcoming the Forces of Oppositions
66) Quenching the Voice of the Avenger
67) Silencing Demonic Prediction & Projection
68) Silencing Your Mocker
69) Understanding the Power of the Holy Ghost
70) Understanding the Baptism of Power
71) The Mystery of the Blood of Jesus
72) Understanding the Mystery of Sanctification
73) Understanding the Power of Holiness
74) Understanding the Forces of Purity & Righteousness
75) Activating the Forces of Vengeance
76) Appreciating the Mystery of Restoration
77) Overcoming the Projection & Prediction of the Enemy
78) Engaging the Mystery of the Blood
79) Commanding the Power of the Speaking Faith
80) Uprooting the Forces Against Your Rising
81) Overcoming Mere Success Syndrome
82) Understanding Divine Sentence
83) Understanding the Mystery of Praise
84) Understanding the Author of Faith
85) The Mystery of the Finisher of Faith
86) Attracting Supernatural Favor

MIRACLE OF GOD MINISTRIES

NIGERIA CRUSADE 2012

MIRACLE OF GOD MINISTRIES
NIGERIA CRUSADE
2012

MIRACLE OF GOD MINISTRIES
NIGERIA CRUSADE 2012

MIRACLE OF GOD MINISTRIES

NIGERIA CRUSADE

2012

MIRACLE OF GOD MINISTRIES

NIGERIA CRUSADE

2012

www.ingramcontent.com/pod-product-compliance
Lightning Source LLC
Chambersburg PA
CBHW021446080526
44588CB00009B/712